WORDS-ON

Contemporary, Traditional, and New Choruses
COMPILED BY KEN BIBLE

Contents

Lillenas Publishing Co.
KANSAS CITY, MO. 64141

WORSHIP AND PRAISE

1

JESUS, NAME ABOVE ALL NAMES
by Naida Hearn

Jesus, name above all names,
Beautiful Savior, glorious Lord.
Emmanuel: God is with us!
Blessed Redeemer, Living Word.

2

HIS NAME IS LIFE
by Carman Licciardello, William J. and Gloria Gaither

His name is Master, Savior, Lion of Judah,
Blessed Prince of Peace.
Shepherd, Fortress, Rock of Salvation,
Lamb of God is He.
Son of David, King of the Ages,
Eternal Life,
Holy Lord of Glory, His name is Life.

3

I EXALT THEE
by Pete Sanchez, Jr.

For Thou, O Lord, art high above all the
    earth;
Thou art exalted far above all gods.
    (Repeat)
I exalt Thee, I exalt Thee,
I exalt Thee, O Lord!
    (Repeat last 2 lines.)

4

HOLY SPIRIT, THOU ART WELCOME
by Dottie Rambo, David Huntsinger

Holy Spirit, Thou art welcome in this place.
Holy Spirit, Thou art welcome in this place.
Omnipotent Father of mercy and grace,
Thou art welcome in this place.

5

HOLY SAVIOR
by Mosie Lister

Holy Savior, Lord, we adore You;
Holy Savior, Jesus, Son of God.

6

ABBA FATHER
by Steve Fry

"Abba Father, Abba Father,"
Deep within my soul I cry.
Abba Father, Abba Father,
I will never cease to love You.

Father, Father, Jehovah Shammah,
You are the One who's standing near.
Abba Father, Abba Father,
I will never cease to love You.

7

OH, HOW HE LOVES YOU AND ME
by Kurt Kaiser

Oh, how He loves you and me;
Oh, how He loves you and me.
He gave His life—what more could He give?
Oh, how He loves you; Oh, how He loves me;
Oh, how He loves you and me.

Jesus to Calv'ry did go,
His love for sinners to show.
What He did there brought hope from
    despair.
Oh, how He loves you; Oh, how He loves me;
Oh, how He loves you and me.

8

HIS NAME IS WONDERFUL
by Audrey Mieir

His name is Wonderful; His name is
    Wonderful;
His name is Wonderful—Jesus, my Lord.
He is the mighty King, Master of ev'rything;
His name is Wonderful—Jesus, my Lord.

He's the great Shepherd, the Rock of all ages,
Almighty God is He.
Bow down before Him, love and adore Him;
His name is Wonderful—Jesus, my Lord.

9

COME CELEBRATE JESUS
by Claire Cloninger, John Rosasco

Come celebrate Jesus, come celebrate Jesus;
The bread and the wine, the moment in time.
Come celebrate Jesus, the Spirit that frees us;
His table has been laid, come now and
    celebrate Him.

10

BECAUSE OF WHO YOU ARE
by Bob Farrell, Billy Smiley

Lord, I praise You because of who You are,
Not because of all the mighty things You've
    done.
Lord, I worship You because of who You are;
You're all the reason that I need to voice my
    praise,
Because of who You are.

11

I LIVE!
by Rich Cook

I live, I live because He is risen;
I live, I live with pow'r over sin.
I live, I live because He is risen;
I live, I live to worship Him.

Thank You, Jesus! Thank You, Jesus!
Because You're alive, because You're alive,
Because You're alive, I live!

12

JESUS, LORD TO ME
by Gary McSpadden, Greg Nelson

Jesus, Jesus, Lord to me;
Master, Savior, Prince of Peace!
Ruler of my heart today,
Jesus, Lord to me.

13

FILL MY CUP, LORD
by Richard Blanchard

Fill my cup, Lord—I lift it up, Lord!
Come and quench this thirsting of my soul.
Bread of heaven, feed me till I want no more;
Fill my cup, fill it up and make me whole!

14

LET THERE BE PRAISE
by Melodie and Dick Tunney

Refrain:
Let there be praise, let there be joy in our
    hearts.
Sing to the Lord, give Him the glory.
Let there be praise, let there be joy in our
    hearts.
Forevermore let His love fill the air, and let
    there be praise.

He inhabits the praise of His people,
And dwells deep within.
The peace that He gives none can equal;
His love, it knows no end.
So lift your voices, with gladness sing;
Proclaim through all the earth
That Jesus Christ is King!
    (Repeat refrain)
When the Spirit of God is within us,
We will overcome.
In our weakness His strength will defend us,
When His praise is on our tongue.
So lift your voices, with gladness sing;
Proclaim through all the earth
That Jesus Christ is King!
    (Repeat refrain)

15

THERE IS A REDEEMER
by Melody Green

There is a Redeemer, Jesus, God's own Son;
Precious Lamb of God, Messiah, Holy One.
Refrain:
Thank You, oh, my Father, for giving us Your
  Son,
And leaving Your Spirit 'til the work on earth
  is done.

Jesus, my Redeemer, name above all names;
Precious Lamb of God, Messiah, O for
  sinners slain.

When I stand in Glory, I will see His face;
There I'll serve my King forever in that holy
  place.

16

HOLY GROUND
by Geron Davis

We are standing on holy ground,
And I know that there are angels all around.
Let us praise Jesus now.
We are standing in His presence on holy
  ground.

17

WE ARE SO BLESSED
*by Greg Nelson, William J. and
Gloria Gaither*

We are so blessed by the gifts from Your
  hand,
I just can't understand why You've loved us
  so much.
We are so blessed we just can't find a way,
Or the words that can say, "Thank You, Lord,
  for Your touch."

When we're empty, You fill us till we
  overflow.
When we're hungry, You feed us and cause us
  to know
We are so blessed; take what we have to
  bring,
Take it all, everything, for we love You so
  much.

18

O COME, LET US ADORE HIM
Traditional

O come, let us adore Him;
O come, let us adore Him;
O come, let us adore Him, Christ the Lord.

We'll praise His name forever . . .

We'll give Him all the glory . . .

For He alone is worthy . . .

19

THE LORD IS LIFTED UP
by Kenny Woods, Billy Crockett

The Lord is lifted up
In majesty and praise.
The earth beholds and bows before
The wonder of His grace.
The Lord is lifted up,
Above creation reigns.
While earthly kingdoms rise and fall,
His holiness remains;
God's holiness remains.

20

ALLELUIA
by Jerry Sinclair

Alleluia, Alleluia, Alleluia, Alleluia,
Alleluia, Alleluia, Alleluia, Alleluia!

He's my Savior . . .

He is worthy . . .

I will praise Him . . .

21

KING OF KINGS
by Sophie Conty, Naomi Batya

King of Kings and Lord of Lords, glory,
  hallelujah!

King of Kings and Lord of Lords, glory,
hallelujah!
Jesus, Prince of Peace, glory, hallelujah!
Jesus, Prince of Peace, glory, hallelujah!
(Repeat)

22

O MAGNIFY THE LORD
by Melodie and Dick Tunney

O magnify, O magnify the Lord with me,
And let us exalt His name together!
O magnify the Lord, O magnify the Lord,
And may His name be lifted high forever.

O worship Him, O worship Christ the Lord
with me,
And let us exalt His name together!
O worship Christ the Lord, O worship Christ
the Lord,
And may His name be lifted high forever.

King of Kings and Lord of Lords,
May His name be lifted high forever!
(Repeat v. 1)

23

O HOW I LOVE JESUS
by Frederick Whitfield, Trad.

O how I love Jesus!
O how I love Jesus!
O how I love Jesus,
Because He first loved me.

24

WE HAVE COME INTO HIS HOUSE
by Bruce Ballinger

We have come into His house
And gathered in His name to worship Him.
(Repeat)
We have come into His house
And gathered in His name to worship Christ
the Lord.
Worship Him, Christ the Lord.

So forget about yourself
And concentrate on Him and worship Him.
(Repeat)
So forget about yourself
And concentrate on Him, and worship
Christ the Lord.
Worship Him, Christ the Lord.

Let us lift up holy hands
And magnify His name and worship Him.
(Repeat)
Let us lift up holy hands
And magnify His name and worship Christ
the Lord.
Worship Him, Christ the Lord.

25

WORSHIP THE KING
by Billy Smiley, Bill George

Come, let us worship the King;
Jesus, the Savior is born.
For the Lord will reign over all the earth.
Come, let us worship the King;
Jesus, the Savior is born.
For the Lord is great and greatly to be praised
Through all the earth.
Let us worship the King.

26 Learn

IT'S TIME TO PRAISE THE LORD
by Bruce and Judi Borneman

Don't you know it's time to praise the Lord
In the sanctuary of His Holy Spirit.
So set your mind on Him,
And let your praise begin,
And the glory of the Lord will fill this place.
Praise the Lord, praise the Lord.

He lives within the praises of His people;
He loves to hear us call upon His name.
So set your mind on Him,
And let your praise begin,
And the glory of the Lord will fill this place.
Praise the Lord, praise the Lord, praise the
Lord.

27

BEAUTIFUL
by Dennis Cleveland

Beautiful, beautiful, Jesus is beautiful,
And Jesus makes beautiful things of my life.
Carefully touching me, causing my eyes to
see,
Jesus makes beautiful things of my life.

28

IN THIS VERY ROOM
by Ron and Carol Harris

In this very room there's quite enough love
for one like me.
And in this very room there's quite enough
joy for one like me.
And there's quite enough hope, and quite
enough power
To chase away any gloom.
For Jesus, Lord Jesus, is in this very room.

In this very room there's quite enough love
for all of us.
And in this very room there's quite enough
joy for all of us.
And there's quite enough hope, and quite
enough power
To share wherever we go.
For Jesus, Lord Jesus, is in this very room.

In this very room there's quite enough love
for all the world.
And in this very room there's quite enough
joy for all the world.
And there's quite enough hope, and quite
enough power
To reach to all of the earth.
For Jesus, Lord Jesus, is in this very room.

29

HONOR THE LORD
by Greg Davis, Greg Fisher

Honor the Lord with your song of praise,
Come before Him with singing.
Lift up your hands and your voices raise;
Honor the Lord with your song of praise.

30

WE BOW DOWN
by Twila Paris

You are Lord of creation and Lord of my life,
Lord of the land and the sea.
You were Lord of the heaven before there was
time,
And Lord of all lords You will be!

We bow down and we worship You, Lord.
We bow down and we worship You, Lord.
We bow down and we worship You, Lord.
Lord of all lords You will be!

You are King of creation and King of my life,
King of the land and the sea.
You were King of the heaven before there was
time,
And King of all kings You will be!
We bow down and we crown You the King.
We bow down and we crown You the King.
We bow down and we crown You the King.
King of all kings You will be!

31

EMMANUEL
by Bob McGee

Emmanuel, Emmanuel,
His name is called Emmanuel:
God with us, revealed in us!
His name is called Emmanuel.

32

CORNERSTONE
by Leon Patillo

I lay in Zion for a foundation, a stone.
I lay in Zion for a foundation, a stone—
A tried stone, a precious cornerstone,
A sure foundation, a sure foundation,
A tried stone, a precious cornerstone.
He that believeth shall, shall not make haste.

33

MAJESTY
by Jack W. Hayford

Majesty, worship His majesty.
Unto Jesus be all glory, honor, and praise.
Majesty, kingdom authority
Flow from His throne unto His own;
His anthem raise.

So exalt, lift up on high the name of Jesus.
Magnify, come glorify Christ Jesus the King.

Majesty, worship His majesty;
Jesus who died, now glorified,
King of all kings.

34

I LOVE HIM
Traditional

I love Him, I love Him
Because He first loved me,
And purchased my salvation on Calv'ry's tree.

35

MY TRIBUTE
by Andraé Crouch

To God be the glory, to God be the glory,
To God be the glory for the things He has
    done.
With His blood He has saved me;
With His power He has raised me;
To God be the glory for the things He has
    done.

Just let me live my life;
Let it be pleasing, Lord, to Thee.
And if I gain any praise,
Let it go to Calvary.

With His blood He has saved me;
With His power He has raised me;
To God be the glory for the things He has
    done.

36

LET'S TALK ABOUT JESUS
Traditional

Let's talk about Jesus—the King of Kings is
    He,
The Lord of Lords supreme through all
    eternity;
The great I AM, the Way, the Truth, the Life,
    the Door—
Let's talk about Jesus more and more.

37

WE WILL GLORIFY
by Twila Paris

We will glorify the King of Kings,
We will glorify the Lamb,
We will glorify the Lord of Lords,
Who is the Great I AM.

Lord Jehovah reigns in majesty;
We will bow before His throne.
We will worship Him in righteousness;
We will worship Him alone.

He is Lord above the universe,
He is Lord of all who live,
He is Lord above the heav'n and earth;
All praise to Him we give.

Oh, hallelujah to the King of Kings,
Hallelujah to the Lamb,
Hallelujah to the Lord of Lords,
Who is the Great I AM.

38

THE LOVE OF GOD
by Frederick M. Lehman

O love of God, how rich and pure,
How measureless and strong!
It shall forevermore endure
The saints' and angels' song.

39

LET THERE BE AN ANOINTING
by Jack Hayford

Let there be an anointing of the Spirit,
Let there be an outpouring of Thy pow'r.
Let there be an overflowing of the love of
    God,
That Thy name be magnified this hour.

Let there be a displaying of Thy glory.
Let there be a revealing of Thy grace.
Let there be an understanding of Thy will
    and way,
That Thy kingdom come within this place.

Let there be an exalting of Christ Jesus.
Let there be an unfolding of the Word.
Let the truth bring liberty of life and health,
That Thy name be magnified as Lord.

40

THE MAJESTY AND GLORY OF YOUR NAME

by Linda Lee Johnson, Tom Fettke

Alleluia, Alleluia!
The majesty and glory of Your name.
Alleluia, Alleluia!
The majesty and glory of Your name.
Alleluia, Alleluia, Alleluia, Alleluia!
Alleluia, Alleluia, Alleluia!

41

SING PRAISE TO THE KING

by Mosie Lister

Sing praise to the King of Kings.
Sing praise to the King of Kings.
Lift high the holy name of Jesus;
Sing praise, praise to the King of Kings.

42

I WILL LIFT MY HEART

by David E. Williams

I will lift my heart in prayer.
I will lift my heart in prayer.
To the God who hears His children praying,
I lift my heart.

I will lift my voice in song.
I will lift my voice in song.
To the God who fills our lives with music,
I lift my voice.

We will lift our hands in praise.
We will lift our hands in praise.
To the God who purchased our redemption,
We lift our praise!

43

THANK YOU, LORD

by Seth and Bessie Sykes

Thank You, Lord, for saving my soul;
Thank You, Lord, for making me whole;
Thank You, Lord, for giving to me
Thy great salvation so rich and free.

44

I LOVE YOU, LORD

by Laurie Klein

I love You, Lord, and I lift my voice
To worship You; O my soul, rejoice!
Take joy, my King, in what You hear;
May it be a sweet, sweet sound in Your ear.

45

WORTHY IS THE LAMB

by Don Wyrtzen

Worthy is the Lamb that was slain,
Worthy is the Lamb that was slain,
Worthy is the Lamb that was slain to receive:
Power and riches and wisdom and strength,
Honor and glory and blessing!
Worthy is the Lamb, worthy is the Lamb,
Worthy is the Lamb that was slain;
Worthy is the Lamb!

46

WE WORSHIP AND ADORE YOU

Unknown

We worship and adore You,
Bowing down before You,
Songs of praises singing,
Hallelujahs ringing.
Hallelujah, hallelujah,
Hallelujah, amen.

47

JESUS, WE JUST WANT TO THANK YOU

by William J. and Gloria Gaither

Jesus, we just want to thank You;
Jesus, we just want to thank You;
Jesus, we just want to thank You,
Thank You for being so good.

Jesus, we just want to praise You . . .
Praise You for being so good.

Jesus, we just want to tell You . . .
We love You for being so good.

Savior, we just want to serve You . . .
Serve You for being so good.

Jesus, we know You are coming . . .
Take us to live in Your home.

48

HIS PRAISE FILLS THE TEMPLE

by Jack Hayford

His praise fills the temple,
His peace fills my heart;
His joy and His glory He did wondrously
  impart.
The bless'd name of Jesus
Brought me freedom from sin;
Now His praise fills the temple
And His Spirit dwells within.

49

HALLELUJAH!

Unknown

Hallelu, hallelu, hallelu, hallelujah!
Praise ye the Lord!
    (Repeat)
Praise ye the Lord, hallelujah!
Praise ye the Lord, hallelujah!
Praise ye the Lord, hallelujah!
Praise Ye the Lord.

50

A PERFECT HEART

by Dony McGuire, Reba Rambo

Bless the Lord who reigns in beauty;
Bless the Lord who reigns in wisdom and
  with pow'r.
Bless the Lord who reigns my life with so
  much love,
He can make a perfect heart.

51

BLESS HIS HOLY NAME

by Andraé Crouch

Bless the Lord, O my soul, and all that is
  within me,
Bless His holy Name.
He has done great things, He has done great
  things,
He has done great things,
Bless His holy Name.
Bless the Lord, O my soul, and all that is
  within me,
Bless His holy Name.

52

I WILL CALL UPON THE LORD

by Michael O'Shields

I will call upon the Lord
Who is worthy to be praised;
So shall I be saved from my enemies.
I will call upon the Lord.
    (Repeat)
The Lord liveth and blessed be the Rock,
And let the God of my salvation be exalted.
The Lord liveth and blessed be the Rock,
And let the God of my salvation be exalted.
    (Repeat last 4 lines)

53

SPIRIT SONG
by John Wimber

O let the Son of God enfold you
With His Spirit and His love;
Let Him fill your heart and satisfy your soul.
O let Him have the things that hold you,
And His Spirit, like a dove,
Will descend upon your life and make you
    whole.

Refrain:
Jesus, O Jesus, come and fill Your lambs.
Jesus, O Jesus, come and fill Your lambs.

O come and sing the song with gladness
As your hearts are filled with joy,
Lift your hands in sweet surrender to His
    name.
O give Him all your tears and sadness;
Give Him all your years of pain,
And you'll enter into life in Jesus' name.
    (Repeat refrain)

54

JESUS IS THE SWEETEST NAME I KNOW
by Lela Long

Jesus is the sweetest name I know,
And He's just the same as His lovely name,
And that's the reason why I love Him so.
Oh, Jesus is the sweetest name I know!

55

GREAT AND WONDERFUL
by Stuart Dauermann

Great and wonderful are Thy wondrous
    deeds,
O Lord God, the Almighty.
Just and true are all Thy ways, O Lord;
King of the ages art Thou.

Who shall not fear and glorify
Thy name, O Lord?
For Thou alone art holy,
Thou alone.

All the nations shall come and worship Thee,
For Thy glory shall be revealed.
Hallelujah! Hallelujah!
Hallelujah! Amen.

56

BLESS THE LORD, O MY SOUL
Unknown

Bless the Lord, O my soul;
Bless the Lord, O my soul;
And all that is within me
Bless His holy name.

57

LET'S JUST PRAISE THE LORD
by William J. and Gloria Gaither

Let's just praise the Lord! Praise the Lord!
Let's just lift our hearts to heaven and praise
    the Lord.
    (Repeat)

58

LORD, WE PRAISE YOU
by Otis Skillings

Lord, we praise You.
Lord, we praise You.
Lord, we praise You.
We praise You, Lord.

Lord, we love You . . .

Alleluia . . .
We give You praise.

59

I'M HUNGRY, LORD
Unknown

I'm hungry, Lord; I'm hungry, Lord;
My soul cries out for Thee.
The Living Bread, the Water of Life,
The One who quickens me.

60

THIS IS MY BODY
by Jack Hayford

This is My body that is broken for you.
This is the covenant that Christ now renews.
My life for yours, that your life may be Mine;
This bread is My body; My blood is this wine.
Eat now and drink, taking life to your soul;

And feast on the promise—let Jesus make
you whole.
Health for your weakness and forgiveness
anew;
Take now, this is My body that is broken for
you.

61

OPEN OUR EYES
by Bob Cull

Open our eyes, Lord, we want to see Jesus;
To reach out and touch Him
And say that we love Him.
Open our ears, Lord, and help us to listen.
Open our eyes, Lord, we want to see Jesus.

62

BEHOLD THE LAMB
by Dottie Rambo

Behold the Lamb! Behold the Lamb!
Slain from the foundation of the world.
For sinners crucified, oh, Holy Sacrifice!
Behold the Lamb of God! Behold the Lamb!

63

HALLOWED BE THE NAME
by Lilly Green

Hallowed be the name of Jesus.
Holy is the name of Jesus.
Other kingdoms rise and fall,
But He reigneth over all.
Hallowed be the name of Jesus.

Worthy is the Lamb, Lord Jesus.
Righteous I can stand in Jesus.
We were chained to death, but then
You raised us up again.
Worthy is the Lamb, Lord Jesus.

64

I WILL ENTER HIS GATES
by Leona Von Brethorst

I will enter His gates with thanksgiving in my
heart;

I will enter His courts with praise.
I will say this is the day that the Lord has
made;
I will rejoice for He has made me glad.
He has made me glad, He has made me glad;
I will rejoice for He has made me glad.
He has made me glad, He has made me glad;
I will rejoice for He has made me glad.

65

GOD IS SO GOOD
Unknown

God is so good, God is so good,
God is so good, He's so good to me!

He cares for me . . . He's so good to me!

I'll do His will . . . He's so good to me!

He is my Lord . . . He's so good to me!

66

I WILL OFFER YOU PRAISE
by Gary Johnson

I will offer You praise when the sun meets the
dew,
And I will offer You praise at the noon's
brightest hue.
I will offer You praise when the starlight is
due;
And if I wake in the night, Lord, I'll still be
praising You.

I will offer You *thanks* . . .
I'll still be *thanking* You.

I will offer You *love* . . .
I'll still be *loving* You.

67

HE IS LIFE
Traditional

He is life unto this soul of mine,
My Jesus, my Jesus.
He is life unto this soul of mine,
Jesus Christ, my Lord divine.
Jesus, Jesus, Jesus, Jesus;
He is life unto this soul of mine,
Jesus Christ, my Lord divine.

68

SING HALLELUJAH (TO THE LORD)
by Linda Stassen

Sing hallelujah to the Lord.
Sing hallelujah to the Lord.
Sing hallelujah, sing hallelujah,
Sing hallelujah to the Lord.

Jesus is risen from the dead . . .

Christ is the Lord of Heav'n and earth . . .

Praise be to God forevermore . . .

Sing hallelujah to the Lord . . .

69

LIFT UP JESUS
by William J. and Gloria Gaither

Oh, lift up Jesus; lift up Jesus;
He's the only One can fill the void in me.
Just lift up Jesus, lift up Jesus;
He's the only One we really need to see.

70

THOU ART WORTHY
by Pauline M. Mills

Thou art worthy, Thou art worthy,
Thou art worthy, O Lord,
To receive glory, glory and honor,
Glory and honor and power.
For Thou hast created, hast all things created;
Thou hast created all things.
And for Thy pleasure they are created,
For Thou art worthy, O Lord.

71

INTO THY PRESENCE
Unknown

Into Thy presence we come;
Not by the works we have done,
But by Thy grace, and Thy grace alone,
Into Thy presence we come.

72

ALLELU, ALLELU
by Dan Whittemore

Refrain:
Allelu, allelu,
Song of my spirit in praise to You.
For all the wonderful things You do,
Allelu, allelu.

Praise Your name, praise Your name;
You bore my penalty and my shame.
For all the promises that I claim,
Allelu, allelu.

God of love, God of love,
Nothing I do makes me worthy of
All that I have in You from above.
God of love, God of love.

Prince of Peace, Prince of Peace.
All my anxiety now has ceased.
The battle's over—I've been released.
Prince of Peace, Prince of Peace.

Holy King, holy King,
Exalted Savior, with joy we sing
Glory to God for the hope You bring.
Holy King, holy King.

73

HE IS LORD
Unknown

He is Lord, He is Lord!
He is risen from the dead and He is Lord!
Ev'ry knee shall bow, ev'ry tongue confess
That Jesus Christ is Lord.

74

HOLY, HOLY
by Jimmy Owens

Holy, holy, holy, holy,
Holy, holy, Lord God Almighty;
And we lift our hearts before You as a token
    of our love,
Holy, holy, holy, holy.

Gracious Father, Gracious Father,
We're so blest to be Your children, Gracious
    Father;
And we lift our heads before You as a token
    of our love,
Gracious Father, Gracious Father.

Precious Jesus, Precious Jesus,
We're so glad that You've redeemed us,
Precious Jesus;
And we lift our hands before You as a token
of our love,
Precious Jesus, Precious Jesus.

Holy Spirit, Holy Spirit,
Come and fill our hearts anew, Holy Spirit;
And we lift our voice before You as a token
of our love,
Holy Spirit, Holy Spirit.

Hallelujah, Hallelujah,
Hallelujah, Hallelujah;
And we lift our hearts before You as a token
of our love,
Hallelujah, Hallelujah.

75

ALLELUIA TO THE KING
by Mosie Lister
Because God is holy, I will bow down before
Him.
Because He is holy, His name I adore.
Because God is worthy, He alone is worthy,
I will lift my voice to praise Him evermore.
Alleluia! Alleluia!
Alleluia! Let the whole world sing.
Alleluia! Alleluia!
Alleluia to the King.

76

HE IS THE WAY
by Otis Skillings
God sent His Son to be our Savior;
God sent His Son to be our Savior;
God sent His Son to be our Savior.
He is the Way; He is the Truth; He is the Life.

'Twas Jesus Christ who came to save the
world . . .

He gave His life that we might be set free . . .

Rose from the grave that we might live
again . . .

He lives today; I know He always will . . .

77

COME INTO HIS PRESENCE
Unknown
Come into His presence singing Alleluia,
Alleluia, alleluia.

Come into His presence singing Jesus is Lord,
Jesus is Lord, Jesus is Lord.

Praise the Lord together singing Worthy the
Lamb,
Worthy the Lamb, worthy the Lamb.

Praise the Lord together singing Glory to
God,
Glory to God, glory to God.

78

THE LORD IS IN THIS PLACE
by Mosie Lister
Surely, surely the Lord himself is in this
place.
Jesus, Jesus, Jesus is here with love and grace.
Pray, brothers, pray;
Pray, sisters, pray;
Pray till the mountains melt away.
For Jesus is near you,
And Jesus will hear you;
For surely the Lord is in this place.

79

CLAP YOUR HANDS
by Jimmy Owens
Clap your hands, all you people;
Shout unto God with a voice of triumph!
Clap your hands, all you people;
Shout unto God with a voice of praise!

Hosanna! Hosanna!
Shout unto God with a voice of triumph!
Praise Him! Praise Him!
Shout unto God with a voice of praise!

80

I SAW THE LORD

Unknown

I saw the Lord, I saw the Lord.
He was high and lifted up
And His train filled the temple;
He was high and lifted up
And His train filled the temple.
The angels cried, "Holy!"
The angels cried, "Holy!"
The angels cried, "Holy is the Lord!"

81

FATHER, I ADORE YOU

by Terrye Coelho

Father, I adore You;
Lay my life before You.
How I love You!

Jesus . . .

Spirit . . .

82

FATHER, WE THANK YOU

by Gary Johnson

Father, we thank You;
Father, we thank You
For giving to us Your Son;
Father, we thank You.

Jesus, we thank You;
Jesus, we thank You
For giving to us Your Spirit;
Jesus, we thank You.

Father, we love You;
Father, we love You
Because You have first loved us;
Father, we love You.

83

BEHOLD

by Stuart Dauermann

Behold, God is my salvation.
I will trust and will not be afraid.
For the Lord my God is my strength and my
  song;
He also has become my salvation.
For the Lord my God is my strength and my
  song;
He also has become my salvation.

84

I WILL SING OF THE MERCIES

Unknown

I will sing of the mrercies of the Lord forever,
I will sing. I will sing.
I will sing of the mercies of the Lord forever,
I will sing of the mercies of the Lord.
With my mouth will I make known.
Thy faithfulness, Thy faithfulness.
With my mouth will I make known
Thy faithfulness to all generations.
I will sing of the mercies of the Lord forever,
I will sing of the mercies of the Lord.

85

THY LOVING KINDNESS

by Hugh Mitchell

Thy loving kindness is better than life.
Thy loving kindness is better than life.
My lips shall praise Thee,
Thus will I bless Thee,
I will lift up my hands unto Thy Name.

I lift my hands, Lord, unto Thy name.
I lift my hands, Lord, unto Thy name.
My lips shall praise Thee,
Thus will I bless thee,
I will lift up my hands unto Thy Name.

86

JESUS, I LOVE YOU

by Otis Skillings

Jesus, I love You, love You, love You.
Jesus, I love You; Jesus, my Lord.

Jesus, I *serve* You . . .

Jesus, I *praise* You . . .

87

THE BOND OF LOVE
by Otis Skillings

We are one in the bond of love;
We are one in the bond of love.
We have joined our spirit with the Spirit of
God;
We are one in the bond of love.

Let us sing now, ev'ry one;
Let us feel His love begun.
Let us join our hands, that the world will
know
We are one in the bond of love.

88

THE HEAVENS DECLARE
by David L. Burkum

Refrain:
The heavens declare the glory of God;
The sky proclaims the work of His hands.
(Repeat)
They speak of the Lord day after day,
Night after night His knowledge display.
The heavens declare the glory of God;
The sky proclaims the work of His hands.
(Repeat refrain)
Their voices go out to all of the earth;
No language is known where they are not
heard.
The heavens declare the glory of God;
The sky proclaims the work of His hands.

89

PRAISE HIM
Traditional

Praise Him, praise Him,
Praise Him in the morning,
Praise Him at the noontime.
Praise Him, praise Him.
Praise Him when the sun goes down.

90

WE'VE COME, O LORD
by Don Neufeld

We've come to seek Your face, O Lord;
We've come to worship You.
We've come to sense Your presence, Lord;
Our weakened faith renew.
We've come to feed upon Your Word,
To gain new strength and pow'r.
We've come to set ourselves apart
For You this quiet hour.

91

EVEN SO, COME
by Gary Johnson

Even so, come, Maranatha;
Come, come, Lord Jesus.
The Spirit and the Bride say, "Come."
Come, Lord Jesus.

Even so, come, Light of men;
Come, come, Lord Jesus.
To those who walk in darkness, come.
Come, Lord Jesus.

Even so, come, by Thy Spirit;
Come, come, Lord Jesus.
Upon our sons and daughters, come.
Come, Lord Jesus.

(Repeat v. 1)

REJOICING AND TESTIMONY

92
SPRING UP, O WELL
Unknown

I've got a river of life flowing out of me;
Makes the lame to walk and the blind to see,
Opens prison doors, sets the captives free.
I've got a river of life flowing out of me.
Spring up, O well, within my soul;
Spring up, O well, and make me whole;
Spring up, O well, and give to me
That life abundantly.

93
I'M IN THIS CHURCH
by Joel Hemphill

I'm in this church, this glorious church;
I didn't join, oh, I was born; I've had a new
  birth!
Some glorious day, gonna sail away;
It's by His grace, not by my works I'm in this
  church!

94
MY SINS ARE GONE
by Helen Griggs

Gone, gone, gone, gone! Yes, my sins are
  gone.
Now my soul is free and in my heart's a song.
Buried in the deepest sea, yes that's good
  enough for me.
I shall live eternally; praise God, my sins are
  gone!

95
DOWN IN MY HEART
by George W. Cooke

I have the joy, joy, joy, joy down in my heart,
Down in my heart, down in my heart.
I have the joy, joy, joy, joy down in my heart,
Down in my heart to stay.

I have the peace that passeth
  understanding . . .
I have the love of Jesus, love of Jesus . . .

96
THE HAPPY SIDE OF LIFE
by Eddie Smith

I've found the happy side of life;
I've found the happy side of life.
With Jesus as my Savior, I've found the way.
Rollin' along, singin' a song
Ev'ry single passing day.
I've found the happy side of life;
I've found the happy side of life.
With Jesus as my Savior, I've found the way.
I've found the happy side of,
I've found the happy side of,
I've found the happy side of life.

97
SAVED TO TELL OTHERS
by Hollywood Gospel Team, Arthur Woolsey

We're saved, saved to tell others
Of the Man of Galilee.
Saved, saved to live daily
For the Christ of Calvary.
Saved, saved to invite you
To His salvation free.
We're saved, saved, saved by His blood
For all eternity.

98
HE IS MY EVERYTHING
Unknown

He is my Ev'rything; He is my All.
He is my Ev'rything, both great and small.
He gave His life for me, made ev'rything new.
He is my Ev'rything. Now, how about you?

99
HIS BANNER OVER ME IS LOVE
Unknown

I'm feasting at His banqueting table;
His banner over me is love.
  (Repeat twice)

His banner over me is love.

He placed my feet on the firm foundation,
His banner . . .

He is the vine and we are the branches, His
banner . . .

100
I'M SO HAPPY
by Stanton W. Gavitt

I'm so happy and here's the reason why—
Jesus took my burdens all away.
Now I'm singing as the days go by—
Jesus took my burdens all away.
Once my heart was heavy with a load of sin;
Jesus took the load and gave me peace
    within.
Now I'm singing as the days go by—
Jesus took my burdens all away.

101
THE LONGER I SERVE HIM
by William J. Gaither

The longer I serve Him, the sweeter He
    grows;
The more that I love Him, more love He
    bestows.
Each day is like heaven, my heart overflows;
The longer I serve Him, the sweeter He
    grows.

102
I'M SO GLAD
Unknown

I'm so glad Jesus lifted me.
I'm so glad Jesus lifted me.
I'm so glad Jesus lifted me;
Singing glory, hallelujah, Jesus lifted me!

I was bound, Jesus set me free.
I was bound, Jesus set me free.
I was bound, Jesus set me free;
Singing glory, hallelujah, Jesus lifted me!

I'll tell the world Jesus lifted me.
I'll tell the world Jesus lifted me.
I'll tell the world Jesus lifted me;
Singing glory, hallelujah, Jesus lifted me!

103
I'VE DISCOVERED THE WAY OF GLADNESS
by Floyd W. Hawkins

I've discovered the way of gladness,
I've discovered the way of joy,
I've discovered relief from sadness:
'Tis a happiness without alloy.
I've discovered the fount of blessing,
I've discovered the living Word.
'Twas the greatest of all discoveries
When I found Jesus, my Lord.

104
ALL BECAUSE OF CALVARY
Not printed due to licensing restrictions.

105
EVERYBODY OUGHT TO KNOW
Unknown

Everybody ought to know, everybody ought
    to know,
Everybody ought to know who Jesus is.
    (Repeat)
He's the Lily of the Valley;
He's the Bright and Morning Star;
He's the fairest of ten thousand;
Everybody ought to know.

106
OH SAY, BUT I'M GLAD
by James P. Sullivan, Mildred Sullivan Lacour

Oh, say, but I'm glad, I'm glad.
Oh, say, but I'm glad.
Jesus has come and my cup's overrun;
Oh, say, but I'm glad.

107
THERE'S A NEW SONG IN MY HEART
by John W. Peterson

There's a new song in my heart
Since the Savior set me free;
There's a new song in my heart—
'Tis a heavenly harmony!
All my sins are washed away
In the blood of Calvary;
O what peace and joy nothing can destroy—
There's a new song in my heart.

108
ISN'T THE LOVE OF JESUS SOMETHING WONDERFUL?
by John W. Peterson

Isn't the love of Jesus something wonderful,
Wonderful, wonderful!
O isn't the love of Jesus something wonderful!
Wonderful it is to me.

109
NEW LIFE!
by John W. Peterson

New life in Christ, abundant and free!
What glories shine, what joys are mine,
What wondrous blessings I see!
My past with its sin, the searching and strife,
Forever gone—there's a bright new dawn!
For in Christ I have found new life!

110
I'M GONNA KEEP ON SINGING
by Andraé Crouch

I'm gonna keep on singing,
I'm gonna keep on shouting,
I'm gonna keep on lifting my voice
And let the world know that Jesus saves.

I'm gonna keep on marching,
I'm gonna keep on fighting,
I'm gonna keep on lifting my voice
And let the world know that Jesus saves.

You trumpets keep on sounding,
You bells keep on ringing,
And ev'rybody keep lifting your voice
And let the world know that Jesus saves.

111
WE HAVE NOT RECEIVED
Adapted, Charles A. Tindley

We have not received the spirit of bondage;
We have not received the spirit of fear.
But by His Spirit we cry, "Abba, Father."
We're joint heirs with Christ
And the children of God.

112
FOR GOD SO LOVED THE WORLD
by Frances Townsend, Alfred B. Smith

For God so loved the world, He gave His only
    Son
To die on Calvary's tree, from sin to set me
    free.
Some day He's coming back; what glory that
    will be!
Wonderful His love to me.

113
THE JOY OF THE LORD
by Alliene G. Vale

The joy of the Lord is my strength;
    (Repeat three times)

He gives me living water and I thirst no
    more;
    (Repeat twice)
The joy of the Lord is my strength.

The word of faith is nigh thee, even in thy
    mouth;
    (Repeat twice)
The joy of the Lord is my strength.

114

THE FAMILY OF GOD

by William J. and Gloria Gaither

I'm so glad I'm a part of the family of God—
I've been washed in the fountain, cleansed by
His blood!
Joint heirs with Jesus as we travel this sod;
For I'm part of the fam'ly, the fam'ly of God.

115

BEHOLD, WHAT MANNER OF LOVE

by Pat Van Tine

Behold, what manner of love the Father has
given unto us.
Behold, what manner of love the Father has
given unto us
That we should be called the sons of God,
That we should be called the sons of God.

116

HAPPINESS

by William J. Gaither

I found happiness, I found peace of mind;
I found the joy of living, perfect love sublime;
I found real contentment, happy living in
accord;
I found happiness all the time, wonderful
peace of mind;
When I found the Lord.

117

SOON AND VERY SOON

by Andraé Crouch

Soon and very soon we are goin' to see the
King.
(Repeat twice)
Hallelujah, Hallelujah, we're goin' to see the
King!

No more cryin' there, we are goin' to see the
King . . .

No more dyin' there, we are going to see the
King . . .

(Repeat v. 1)
Hallelujah, Hallelujah, Hallelujah, Hallelujah!

118

COMING AGAIN

by Mosie Lister

Jesus is coming; Jesus is coming;
Jesus is coming. He's coming again.

In clouds of glory, bright clouds of glory,
In clouds of glory He's coming again.

We'll rise to meet Him, rise up to meet Him;
We'll rise to meet Him. He's coming again.

We shall be like Him; we shall be like Him;
We shall be like Him. He's coming again.

Oh, hallelujah! Oh, hallelujah!
Oh, hallelujah! He's coming again.

119

BECAUSE HE LIVES

Not printed due to licensing restrictions.

120

HE'S ALL I NEED

Traditional

He's all I need, He's all I need;
Jesus is all I need.
He's all I need, He's all I need;
Jesus is all I need.

He's real to me, He's real to me;
Jesus is real to me.
He's real to me, He's real to me;
Jesus is real to me.

121

THIS IS THE DAY
by Les Garrett

This is the day, this is the day
That the Lord has made, that the Lord has
made.
We will rejoice, we will rejoice
And be glad in it, and be glad in it.

This is the day that the Lord has made;
We will rejoice and be glad in it.
This is the day, this is the day
That the Lord has made.

122

I AM LOVED
Not printed due to licensing restrictions.

123

ISN'T HE WONDERFUL
Traditional

Isn't He wonderful, wonderful, wonderful;
Isn't Jesus my Lord wonderful!
Eyes have seen, ears have heard;
'Tis recorded in God's Word.
Isn't Jesus my Lord wonderful!

124

GO, TELL IT ON THE MOUNTAIN
Spiritual

Go, tell it on the mountain,
Over the hills and ev'rywhere.
Go, tell it on the mountain
That Jesus Christ is born.

125

THE TREES OF THE FIELD
by Steffi Geiser Rubin, Stuart Dauermann

You shall go out with joy and be led forth
with peace.
The mountains and the hills will break forth
before you;
There'll be shouts of joy, and all the trees of
the field
Will clap, will clap their hands.

And all the trees of the field will clap their
hands,
The trees of the field will clap their hands.
The trees of the field will clap their hands
While you go out with joy.
(Repeat 1st 4 lines)

126

EVERY DAY WITH JESUS
by Robert C. and Wendell P. Loveless

Every day with Jesus
Is sweeter than the day before;
Every day with Jesus,
I love Him more and more.
Jesus saves and keeps me,
And He's the One I'm waiting for.
Every day with Jesus
Is sweeter than the day before.

127

IT IS FINISHED
by Phil Naish, Scott Wesley Brown

It is finished, Christ has won!
It was written of God's Son!
For, behold, the Lamb has fulfilled God's
plan;
And it is finished, and He has just begun!

128

SWEETER AS THE YEARS GO BY
by Lelia N. Morris

Sweeter as the years go by,
Sweeter as the years go by;
Richer, fuller, deeper,
Jesus' love is sweeter,
Sweeter as the years go by.

129
SOMETHING BEAUTIFUL
by William J. and Gloria Gaither

Something beautiful, something good;
All my confusion He understood.
All I had to offer Him was brokenness and
strife,
But He made something beautiful of my life.

130
I'VE GOT PEACE LIKE A RIVER
Spiritual

I've got peace like a river,
I've got peace like a river,
I've got peace like a river in my soul.
(Repeat)

I've got love like an ocean . . .

I've got joy like a fountain . . .

131
ALIVE UNTO GOD
by Gary Moore

Alive unto God am I, and happy and free.
I'm following Christ the King; new purpose I
see.
Committed to this holy way, my pleasure to
do His will.
Alive unto God am I, and willing to go
To those who are lost in sin and waiting to
know
That life can be lived anew when you're alive
unto God!
Come alive unto God!
Christ alone is able to set you free.

132
CHRIST FOR ME!
by Alex Burns

Christ for me, yes, it's Christ for me!
He's my Savior, my Lord and King—
I'm so happy I shout and sing!
Christ for me, yes, it's Christ for me!
Every day as I go my way
It is Christ for me!

133
THE WINDOWS OF HEAVEN ARE OPEN
Unknown

The windows of heaven are open,
The blessings are falling tonight;
There's joy, joy, joy in my soul
Since Jesus made ev'rything right.
I gave Him my old, tattered garments;
He gave me a robe of pure white.
I'm feasting on honey from Canaan,
And that's why I'm happy tonight.

134
THINGS ARE DIFFERENT NOW
by Stanton W. Gavitt

Things are diff'rent now,
Something happened to me
When I gave my heart to Jesus.
Things are diff'rent now—
I was chang'd, it must be,
When I gave my heart to Him.
Things I loved before have passed away,
Things I love far more have come to stay;
Things are different now,
Something happened that day
When I gave my heart to Him.

135
WHEN I MET THE MAN OF CALVARY
by Gary Moore

When I met the Man of Calvary,
He gave life to me!
Then I let the Spirit have control,
His only to be.
I've surrendered all my talents now;
To Him I have made this vow:
His guidance I will allow;
Myself to deny!
Now abundant life He gives to me,
New joy ev'ry day!
From the folly of this world I'm free,
For Christ is the Way.
Turn back from my Lord? Well, why?
Alive unto God am I!
In the center of His will I'll stay
Till Jesus I see!

136

LIFE IS A SYMPHONY

by Beatrice Bush Bixler

Life is a symphony since the Man of Galilee
Changed my discords into song,
Made life sweet the whole day long.
Life is a symphony, praise the Man of Galilee!
No more a stranger—He is the arranger
Of my symphony.

137

I CAN, I WILL, I DO BELIEVE

by Eliza H. Hamilton, J. H. Stockton, Traditional

I can, I will, I do believe;
I can, I will, I do believe;
I can, I will, I do believe
That Jesus saves me now.

He takes me as I am;
He takes me as I am.
He brings His free salvation to me,
And takes me as I am.

138

GLORY HALLELUJAH!

by Leland Green, Norah E. Burne

Glory, hallelujah! Christ has set me free;
Glory, hallelujah! A new life now I see.
My sins are all forgiven, I'm on my way to heaven,
To live eternally.
Glory, hallelujah! He's coming soon for me!

DISCIPLESHIP

139

PEOPLE NEED THE LORD

by Greg Nelson, Phill McHugh

People need the Lord, people need the Lord.
At the end of broken dreams He's the open door.
People need the Lord, people need the Lord.
When will we realize that people need the Lord.

140

MY HANDS BELONG TO YOU

by Anne Weber, Frank Hernandez

My hands belong to You, Lord;
My hands belong to You.
I lift them up to You, Lord,
And sing hallelujah.
I lift them up to You, Lord,
And sing hallelujah.

My *voice* belongs to You . . . I lift *it* up to You . . .

My *heart* belongs to You . . . I lift *it* up to You . . .

141

MY DESIRE

by Lillian Plankenhorn

My desire—to be like Jesus;
My desire—to be like Him!
His Spirit fill me, His love o'erwhelm me;
In deed and word to be like Him.

142

I'LL BE TRUE, PRECIOUS JESUS

Unknown

I'll be true, precious Jesus, I'll be true.
I'll be true, precious Jesus, I'll be true.
There's a race to be run; there's a vict'ry to be won.
Ev'ry hour, by Thy power, I'll be true.

I'll go through, precious Jesus . . .

143

MORE THAN CONQUERORS

by Bill and Janny Grein

We've been made more than conquerors,
Overcomers in this life.
We've been made victorious
Through the blood of Jesus Christ.

144

WHATEVER IT TAKES

by Lanny and Marietta Wolfe

Whatever it takes to draw closer to You, Lord;
That's what I'll be willing to do.
For whatever it takes to be more like You,
That's what I'll be willing to do.
I'll trade sunshine for rain, comfort for pain;
That's what I'll be willing to do.
For whatever it takes for my will to break,
That's what I'll be willing to do.

145

WE ARE HIS HANDS

by Mark Gersmehl

We are His hands, we are His feet;
We are His people, children of the Lord.
We share the hope, we share the dream;
Believers in Jesus, children of the King!

146

JESUS IS LORD

by Ed Seabough, Otis Skillings

With my heart I believe, Jesus Christ is Lord;
And that Jesus rose again, Jesus Christ is Lord.
With my lips I confess, Jesus Christ is Lord;
And I, too, shall live again, Jesus Christ is Lord.
Jesus is Lord, Lord of my life;
Jesus is Lord, Lord of my life.
Jesus is Lord, Lord of my life;
Jesus is Lord.

147

JESUS IS LORD OF ALL

by William J. and Gloria Gaither

All my tomorrows, all my past;
Jesus is Lord of all.
I've quit my struggles, contentment at last;
Jesus is Lord of all.

Refrain:
King of kings, Lord of lords;
Jesus is Lord of all.
All my possessions and all my life;
Jesus is Lord of all.

All of my conflicts, all my thoughts;
Jesus is Lord of all.
His love wins the battles I could not have fought;
Jesus is Lord of all.

All of my longings, all my dreams;
Jesus is Lord of all.
All of my failures His power redeems;
Jesus is Lord of all.

148

SEEK YE FIRST
by Karen Lafferty

Seek ye first the kingdom of God
And His righteousness;
And all these things shall be added unto you.
Hallelu, Hallelujah.

Ask and it shall be given unto you;
Seek and you shall find;
Knock and it shall be opened unto you.
Hallelu, Hallelujah.

149

LORD, BE GLORIFIED
by Bob Kilpatrick

In my life, Lord, be glorified, be glorified,
In my life, Lord, be glorified today.

In your church, Lord, be glorified, be
glorified,
In your church, Lord, be glorified today.

150

IS THERE ANYTHING I CAN DO FOR YOU?
by Dottie Rambo, David Huntsinger

Is there anything I can do for You?
Anything I can do?
For all the things You've done for me,
Is there anything I can do?
I'm willing to be used, dear Lord,
Whate'er the price may be.
So if there's anything I can do for You,
Just make it known to me.

Is there anything I can be for You?
Anything I can be?
For all the things You've been to me,
Is there anything I can be?
I'm willing to be used, dear Lord,
Whate'er the price may be.
So if there's anything I can be for You,
Just make it known to me.

Is there anywhere I can go for You?
Anywhere I can go?
Forsaking all to follow Thee,
Is there anywhere I can go?
I'm willing to be used, dear Lord,
Whate'er the price may be.
So if there's anywhere I can go for You,
Just make it known to me.

151

GOIN' TO BUILD MY LIFE
by Dick Anthony

Goin' to build my life on the Word of God;
Goin' to turn my feet in the narrow way
That the saints have trod.
Goin' to set my heart on things above,
And tell the world that I am full of the
Savior's love.

Goin' to tune my ears to the Spirit's voice;
Goin' to pray that He will lead my life
In His holy choice.
Goin' to use my hands the way He plans,
And daily try my best to do what the Lord
commands.

Goin' to tell my friends 'bout the Jesus way;
Goin' to let them know that He can change
The night to day.
Goin' to use my time in things divine,
And show the world that I am His and He is
mine.

152

I WILL SERVE THEE
by William J. and Gloria Gaither

I will serve Thee because I love Thee;
You have given life to me.
I was nothing before You found me;
You have given life to me.
Heartaches, broken pieces,
Ruined lives are why You died on Calvary.
Your touch was what I longed for;
You have given life to me.

153

WITH ETERNITY'S VALUES IN VIEW
by Al Smith

With eternity's values in view, Lord;
With eternity's values in view—
May I do each day's work for Jesus
With eternity's values in view.

154

THIS IS MY PRAYER
by Doug Holck

I want to love You, Lord;
I want to serve You, Lord;
I want to please You, Lord;
This is my pray'r.
  (Repeat)

155

WE WILL STAND
by Russ and Tori Taff, James Hollihan

You're my brother, you're my sister,
So take me by the hand;
Together we will work until He comes.
There's no foe that can defeat us
When we're walking side by side;
As long as there is love, we will stand.

156

NOW WALK WITH GOD
by Otis Skillings

On God's holy Word I challenge you
To give to the Lord your life anew.
My friend, make your choice; He waits for you,
For this is the moment of truth.
Now walk with God and He will be your dearest Friend,
Where'er you go, in ev'rything you do.
And may your life reflect His love to ev'ryone.
Now walk with God and He will walk with you.

157

INTO THE WORD AND ON TO THE WORLD
by Fred Parker, Eleanor Whitsett

Into the Word and on to the world,
This be our banner proudly unfurled;
Let all our strength 'gainst the foe be hurled.
Go in the pow'r of the Spirit.
Into the Word, His workmen to be;
On to the world that Christ men may see,
Telling the truth that from sin sets free!
Take the Word to the world today.

158

I LOVE YOU WITH THE LOVE OF THE LORD
by James Gilbert

I love you with the love of the Lord,
Yes, I love you with the love of the Lord.
I can see in you the glory of my King,
And I love you with the love of the Lord.

159

ALL POWER IS GIVEN UNTO ME
by James McGranahan

All pow'r is given unto Me,
All pow'r is given unto Me;
Go ye into all the world and preach the gospel
And, lo, I am with you alway.

160

HE'S STILL WORKIN' ON ME
by Joel Hemphill

He's still workin' on me
To make me what I ought to be;
It took Him just a week to make the moon and stars,
The sun and the earth and Jupiter and Mars.
How loving and patient He must be!
He's still workin' on me.

161

SPIRIT OF THE LIVING GOD
by Daniel Iverson

Spirit of the living God, fall fresh on me.
Spirit of the living God, fall fresh on me.
Melt me, mold me, fill me, use me.
Spirit of the living God, fall fresh on me.

162

LORD, LAY SOME SOUL UPON MY HEART
by Leon Tucker, Ira D. Sankey

Lord, lay some soul upon my heart
And love that soul through me;
And may I gladly do my part
To win that soul for Thee.

163

WE SHALL OVERCOME
by Jack Hayford

We shall overcome, we shall overcome
By the Word of God and the blood of the
  Lamb
And the name of our Lord Jesus Christ.
  (Repeat)
By the Word and the blood and the name of
  our Lord Jesus Christ.

164

2 CORINTHIANS 3:18
Unknown

From glory to glory He's changing me,
Changing me, changing me;
His likeness and image to perfect in me—
The love of God shown to the world.
For He's changing, changing me
From earthly things into heavenly;
His likeness and image to perfect in me—
The love of God shown to the world.

165

LET THE BEAUTY OF JESUS BE SEEN IN ME
by Albert Orsborn, Tom Jones

Let the beauty of Jesus be seen in me—
All His wonderful passion and purity!
O Thou Spirit divine,
All my nature refine
Till the beauty of Jesus be seen in me.

166

WE ARE THE BODY OF THE LORD
by Linda Lee Johnson, Tom Fettke

We are the body of the Lord;
We are the body of the Lord.
United in Christ and working together,
We are the body of the Lord.

We are the temple of the Lord;
We are the temple of the Lord.
United in love and growing together,
We are the temple of the Lord.

167

WHISPER A PRAYER
Unknown

Whisper a prayer in the morning,
Whisper a prayer at noon,
Whisper a prayer in the evening
To keep your heart in tune.

God answers prayer in the morning,
God answers prayer at noon,
God answers prayer in the evening;
He'll keep your heart in tune.

Jesus may come in the morning,
Jesus may come at noon,
Jesus may come in the evening;
So keep your heart in tune.

168

MORE OF YOU
by Gary S. Paxton, William J. and Gloria Gaither

More of You, more of You;
I've had all but what I need—just more of
  You.
Of things I've had my fill,
And yet I hunger still.
Empty and bare, Lord, hear my prayer for
  more of You.

169

NOT MY WILL

Unknown

Not my will but Thine be done,
But let the fullness of the Son
Rule within this life that I have offered Thee.
Until ev'rything I do.
Becomes the thing that pleases You.
Abba, Father, I would be a son indeed.

170

CLEAN HANDS, PURE HEART

by John Slick, Mark Gersmehl

Clean hands, a pure heart consecrated to You;
Open, broken in all I say and do.
Oh, dear Lord, give me clean hands,
A pure heart shining for You.

171

INTO MY HEART

Not printed due to licensing restrictions.

172

ABOVE ALL ELSE

by John W. Peterson

Above all else the world needs Jesus,
As shadows fall and hopes grow dim.
He is the best of earth's possessions;
Above all else the world needs Him.
For He can lift a soul from dark despair,
Save from sin and answer pray'r.
There is not another friend like Jesus!
Above all else the world needs Jesus;
Above all else the world needs Him.

173

HIS

by Don and Virginia Poplin Cowley

His is my soul, redeemed from all sin.
His is my heart, purified within.
His is my life, transformed from above;
His my whole being—an offering of love!

174

O TO BE LIKE THEE

by Thomas O. Chisholm, William J. Kirkpatrick

Oh, to be like Thee! Oh, to be like Thee,
Blessed Redeemer, pure as Thou art!
Come in Thy sweetness, come in Thy
fullness;
Stamp Thine own image deep on my heart.

175

I HAVE DECIDED TO FOLLOW JESUS

Unknown

I have decided to follow Jesus;
(Repeat twice)
No turning back, no turning back!

Should no one join me, still I will follow;
(Repeat twice)
No turning back, no turning back!

The world behind me, the cross before me;
(Repeat twice)
No turning back, no turning back!

176

TO BE LIKE JESUS

by John Gowans, John Larsson

To be like Jesus! This hope possesses me.
In ev'ry thought and deed, this is my aim, my
creed:
To be like Jesus! This hope possesses me.
His Spirit helping me, like Him I'll be.

177

LET ME BURN OUT FOR THEE

by Bessie F. Hatcher

Let me burn out for Thee, dear Lord;
Burn and wear out for Thee.
Don't let me rust, or my life be
A failure, my God, to Thee.
Use me and all I have, dear Lord,
And get me so close to Thee
That I feel the throb of the great heart of
God,
Until I burn out for Thee.

178

MAKE ME A SERVANT
by Kelly Willard

Make me a servant, humble and meek;
Lord, let me lift up those who are weak;
And may the pray'r of my heart always be:
Make me a servant, make me a servant,
Make me a servant today.

179

GOD CALLS US
by Linda Rebuck, Tom Fettke

Because so many need to know,
It's up to you and me to go.
Because so many need to know,
God calls us, God calls us.

Because so many need to see
That God alone can make them free.
Because so many need to see,
God calls us, God calls us.

Because so many need to hear,
I want to be a volunteer.
Because so many need to hear,
God calls us, God calls us.

180

JUST A CLOSER WALK WITH THEE
Traditional

I am weak but Thou art strong;
Jesus, keep me from all wrong.
I'll be satisfied as long
As I walk, let me walk close to Thee.

Just a closer walk with Thee;
Grant it, Jesus, is my plea.
Daily walking close to Thee,
Let it be, dear Lord, let it be.

181

PRAY FOR ME
by Dan Whittemore

Pray for me, I'll pray for you
That we be filled with the knowledge of His
will.

In all wisdom and spiritual understanding,
That we might walk in a way that pleases
God.

182

LORD, I WANT TO BE A CHRISTIAN
Spiritual

Lord, I want to be a Christian
In my heart, in my heart.
Lord, I want to be a Christian in my heart.
In my heart, in my heart;
Lord, I want to be a Christian in my heart.

Lord, I want to be more loving . . .

Lord, I want to be more holy . . .

Lord, I want to be like Jesus . . .

183

TO BE LIKE JESUS
Unknown

To be like Jesus, to be like Jesus—
All I ask, to be like Him.
All through life's journey from earth to glory,
All I ask, to be like Him.

184

LEAD ME TO SOME SOUL TODAY
Not printed due to licensing restrictions.

185

YOUR LOVE COMPELS ME
by Doug Holck

Your love compels me, Lord,
To give as You would give,
To speak as You would speak,
To live as You would live.
Your love compels me, Lord,
To see as You would see,
To serve as You would serve,
To be what You would be.

186

WE'LL WORK TILL JESUS COMES
by Elizabeth Mills, William Miller

We'll work till Jesus comes.
We'll work till Jesus comes.
We'll work till Jesus comes,
And we'll be gathered home.

187

TO BE USED OF GOD
by Audrey Mieir

To be used of God to speak, to sing, to pray.
To be used of God to show someone the way.
Oh, how I long to feel the touch of His
  consuming fire.
To be used of God is my desire.

188

THAT THE WORLD MAY KNOW
by Sue Caudill

I want the world to know that Jesus loves
  them so.
I want His life and cleansing pow'r to flow
  through me.
If we will join our hands and do as He
  commands,
Then together we'll reach out an arm of love.
I want the world to see Jesus in you and me,
In perfect unity; that the world may know!

189

TEACH ME, LORD
by Linda Rebuck, Tom Fettke

Teach me, Lord; teach me, Lord;
Teach me to do Your will.
Teach me, Lord; teach me, Lord;
Teach me to trust and obey.
I will listen as You speak in Your still, small
  voice;
As You teach me each day to make the right
  choice.
(Repeat 1st 4 lines)

190

ALWAYS REMEMBER
by Andraé Crouch

Always remember Jesus, Jesus;
Always remember Jesus, Jesus;
Always keep Him on your mind.

191

NOTHING BETWEEN
by C. A. Tindley

Nothing between my soul and the Savior,
So that His blessed face may be seen.
Nothing preventing the least of His favor.
Keep the way clear: let nothing between.

192

NOT MY WILL, BUT THINE
by Hugh C. Benner

Not my will, but Thine; not my will, but
  Thine;
Not my will but Thy will be done, Lord, in
  me.
May Thy Spirit divine fill this being of mine.
Not my will, but Thy will be done, Lord, in
  me.

193

SO SEND I YOU
by Otis Skillings

The harvest is great, but the workers are few;
So send I you.
I have ordained and chosen you;
So send I you.
You are my witness at home and abroad;
So send I you.
Preaching with power the kingdom of God;
So send I you.
Unto the uttermost part of the earth,
Proclaiming the message 'til all men have
  heard.
As the Father hath sent me,
So send I you.

194

SHARE HIS LOVE

by William J. Reynolds

Share His love by telling what the Lord has
 done for you;
Share His love by sharing of your faith;
And show the world that Jesus Christ is real
 to you
Ev'ry moment, ev'ry day.

195

EVERY MOMENT OF EVERY DAY

by Norman J. Clayton

Only to be what He wants me to be,
Ev'ry moment of every day.
Yielded completely to Jesus alone,
Ev'ry step of this pilgrim way.
Just to be clay in the Potter's hands,
Ready to do what His Word commands.
Only to be what He wants me to be,
Ev'ry moment of ev'ry day.

196

THE GREATEST THING

by Mark Pendergrass

The greatest thing in all my life is knowing
 You;
The greatest thing in all my life is knowing
 You.
I want to know You more, I want to know
 You more.
The greatest thing in all my life is knowing
 You.

The greatest thing in all my life is loving You;
The greatest thing in all my life is loving You.
I want to love You more, I want to love You
 more.
The greatest thing in all my life is loving You.

The greatest thing in all my life is serving
 You;
The greatest thing in all my life is serving
 You.
I want to serve You more, I want to serve You
 more.

The greatest thing in all my life is serving
You.

197

I MUST HAVE JESUS

Traditional

I must have Jesus in my whole life;
I must have Jesus in my life.
In my walking, in my talking,
In my sleeping, in my waking;
I must have Jesus in my life.

I have Christ Jesus in my whole life;
I have Christ Jesus in my life.
In my walking, in my talking,
In my sleeping, in my waking;
I have Christ Jesus in my life.

198

I LIVE BY FAITH

by C. C. Dunbar

I live by faith in Him who died;
With Him I have been crucified.
I live and yet it is not I,
But Christ who lives in me.

199

LET THEM KNOW

by Lanny and Marietta Wolfe

Let them know, let them know;
Tell them Jesus loves them so;
Loves them so much that to Calvary He
 would go.
Let them know, let them know
That they, too, can go
To live forevermore with Jesus.
Let them know, let them know.

200

LITTLE BY LITTLE

Unknown

Little by little He's changing me,
Line after line until I can see,
Precept on precept until I am free;
Jesus is changing me.

201
I KNOW THE LORD WILL MAKE A WAY
Unknown

I know the Lord will make a way for me;
I know the Lord will make a way for me.
If I live a holy life,
Shun the wrong and do the right,
I know the Lord will make a way for me.

I want the Lord to have His way with me;
I want the Lord to have His way with me.

Tho' the need be great or small,
I would yield to Him my all,
I want the Lord to have His way with me.

202
KEEP ME TRUE
Unknown

Keep me true, Lord Jesus, keep me true.
Keep me true, Lord Jesus, keep me true.
There's a race that must be run;
There's a vict'ry to be won.
Ev'ry hour, by Thy pow'r, keep me true.

ASSURANCE AND FAITH

203
BE STILL AND KNOW
Unknown

Be still and know that I am God.
   (Repeat twice)

I am the Lord that healeth thee . . .

In Thee, O Lord, I put my trust . . .

204
IN HIS TIME
by Diane Ball

In His time, in His time,
He makes all things beautiful in His time.
Lord, please show me ev'ry day
As You're teaching me Your way,
That You do just what You say in Your time.

In Your time, in Your time,
You make all things beautiful in Your time.
Lord, my life to You I bring;
May each song I have to sing
Be to You a lovely thing in Your time.

205
GOD IS STILL ON THE THRONE
by Mrs. F. W. Suffield

God is still on the throne,
And He will remember His own.
Though trials may press us and burdens
   distress us, He never will leave us alone.
God is still on the throne;

He never forsaketh His own.
His promise is true; He will not forget you.
God is still on the throne.

206
LOOKIN' FOR THE CITY
by Beverly Darnall, Melodie and Dick Tunney

I'm lookin' for the city with the true
   foundation:
A home in the heavens not made by hands.
Its designer and builder is the Lord of the
   ages;
He prepared it for me before the world began.

207
GOD CAN DO ANYTHING BUT FAIL
by Ira F. Stanphill

God can do anything, anything, anything;
God can do anything but fail.
He can save, He can keep, He can cleanse,
   and He will;
God can do anything but fail.
He's the Alpha and Omega, the beginning
   and the end;
He's the fairest of ten thousand to my soul.
God can do anything, anything, anything;
God can do anything but fail.

208

I SHALL NOT BE MOVED

Traditional

Glory, hallelujah! I shall not be moved.
Anchored in Jehovah, I shall not be moved.
Just like a tree that's planted by the waters,
I shall not be moved.

Refrain:
I shall not be, I shall not be moved.
I shall not be, I shall not be moved.
Just like a tree that's planted by the waters,
I shall not be moved.

In His love abiding, I shall not be moved.
And in Him confiding, I shall not be moved.
Just like a tree that's planted by the waters,
I shall not be moved.

Tho' the tempest rages, I shall not be moved.
On the Rock of Ages, I shall not be moved.
Just like a tree that's planted by the waters,
I shall not be moved.

209

THESE TIMES—GOD IS ABLE

by Ron Lush, Mosie Lister

These times God is able. These times God is able.
These times God is able to carry you through.

These times God is willing. These times God is willing.
These times God is willing to carry you through.

These times I will trust Him. These times I will trust Him.
These times I will trust Him; He'll carry me through.

210

PEACE IN THE MIDST OF THE STORM

by Stephen R. Adams

There is peace in the midst of my storm-tossed life;
Oh, there's an Anchor, there's a Rock to cast my faith upon.
Jesus rides in my vessel, so I'll fear no alarm;
He gives me peace in the midst of my storm!

211

LISTEN

Listen; everybody listen.
Listen; everybody listen.
Listen; everybody listen.
Come to Christ today.

Listen; everybody listen.
Listen; everybody listen.
Listen; everybody listen.
He will hear you pray.

Listen; everybody listen.
Listen; everybody listen.
Listen; everybody listen.
Come to Christ today.
He will hear you pray.
Come to Christ today.

212

HE'S ABLE

by Paul E. Paino

He's able, He's able, I know He's able;
I know my Lord is able to carry me through.
  (Repeat)
He healed the brokenhearted and set the captive free;
He made the lame to walk again and caused the blind to see.
He's able, He's able, I know He's able;
I know my Lord is able to carry me through.

213

I JUST KEEP TRUSTING MY LORD

by John W. Peterson

I just keep trusting my Lord as I walk along;
I just keep trusting my Lord and He gives a song.
Tho' the stormclouds darken the sky o'er the heav'nly trail,
I just keep trusting my Lord—He will never fail!
He's a faithful Friend, such a faithful Friend,
I can count on Him to the very end.
Tho' the stormclouds darken the sky o'er the heav'nly trail,
I just keep trusting my Lord—He will never fail!

214

HE'S GOT THE WHOLE WORLD IN HIS HANDS

Spiritual

He's got the whole world in His hands;
He's got the whole world in His hands;
He's got the whole world in His hands.
He's got the whole world in His hands.

He's got the wind and rain in His hands . . .
He's got the whole world in His hands.

He's got you and me in His hands . . .
He's got the whole world in His hands.

He's got ev'rybody in His hands . . .
He's got the whole world in His hands.

215

NO, NEVER ALONE

Unknown

No, never alone; no, never alone.
He promised never to leave me;
He'll claim me for His own.
No, never alone; no, never alone.
He promised never to leave me,
Never to leave me alone.

216

MY LORD KNOWS THE WAY

by Sidney E. Cox

My Lord knows the way thro' the wilderness;
All I have to do is follow.
(Repeat)
Strength for today is mine all the way,
And all I need for tomorrow!
(Repeat 1st 2 lines)

217

KUM-BA-YAH

Traditional

Refrain:
Kum-ba-yah, my Lord, Kum-ba-yah.
Kum-ba-yah, my Lord, Kum-ba-yah.
Kum-ba-yah, my Lord, Kum-ba-yah.
O Lord, Kum-ba-yah.

Someone's crying, Lord; Kum-ba-yah.
Someone's crying, Lord; Kum-ba-yah.
Someone's crying, Lord; Kum-ba-yah.
O Lord, Kum-ba-yah.

Someone's praying, Lord . . .

Someone's singing, Lord . . .

218

FAITH, MIGHTY FAITH, THE PROMISE SEES

by Charles Wesley, unknown composer

Faith, mighty faith, the promise sees
And looks to that alone;
Laughs at impossibilities
And cries: "It shall be done!"
And cries: "It shall, it shall be done!"
And cries: "It shall, it shall be done!"
Laughs at impossibilities
And cries: "It shall be done!"

219

NOT BY MIGHT

by Almeda Herrick

"Not by might, not by pow'r,
But by My Spirit," saith the Lord of Hosts.
"Not by might, not by pow'r,
But by My Spirit," saith the Lord.
This mountain shall be removed;
This mountain shall be removed;
This mountain shall be removed
"By My Spirit," saith the Lord.
"Not by might, not by pow'r,
But by My Spirit," saith the Lord.

220

ALL YOUR ANXIETY

by Edward Henry Joy

All our anxiety, all your care,
Bring to the mercy seat—leave it there.
Never a burden He cannot bear,
Never a friend like Jesus!

221

THROUGH IT ALL
by Andraé Crouch

Through it all, through it all,
Oh, I've learned to trust in Jesus;
I've learned to trust in God.
Through it all, through it all,
Oh, I've learned to depend upon His Word.

222

LISTEN, JESUS IS CALLING YOU
Traditional

Listen, Jesus is calling you,
Calling you, calling you.
Come to Him, He will your heart renew;
Calling, calling you.

223

WITH GOD NOTHING IS IMPOSSIBLE
by Doug Holck

With God there is nothing impossible.
With God there is nothing that He cannot do.
With God there is nothing impossible;
There's nothing that He cannot do.

224

REACH OUT AND TOUCH THE LORD
by Bill Harmon

Reach out and touch the Lord as He walks
by.
You'll find He's not too busy to hear your cry.
He's passing by this moment your needs to
supply.
Reach out and touch the Lord as He walks
by.

225

WHEN WE SEE CHRIST
by Esther Kerr Rusthoi

It will be worth it all when we see Jesus;
Life's trials will seem so small when we see
Christ!
One glimpse of His dear face all sorrow will
erase;
So bravely run the race till we see Christ.

226

IT MATTERS TO HIM
by Audrey Mieir

It matters to Him about you;
Your heartaches, your sorrow He shares.
Regardless of what you may do,
He wants you, He loves you, He cares.
Oh, yes, it matters to Him about you;
Believe it because it is true.
Cling to His hand, He'll understand;
For it matters to Him about you.

227

COME, HOLY SPIRIT
by William J. and Gloria Gaither

Come, Holy Spirit, I need You;
Come, sweet Spirit, I pray.
Come, in Your strength and Your power;
Come, in Your own gentle way.

228

GOD SAID IT, I BELIEVE IT, THAT SETTLES IT
by Stephen R. Adams, Gene Braun

God said it and I believe it,
And that settles it for me!
(Repeat)
Though some may doubt that His Word is
true,
I've chosen to believe it; now how about you?
(Repeat 1st 2 lines)

229

PHILIPPIANS 4:13

by Homer W. Grimes

I can do all things thro' Christ who
  strengtheneth me.
I can do all things thro' Christ who
  strengtheneth me.
Day by day, hour by hour,
I am kept by His pow'r.
I can do all things thro' Christ who
  strengtheneth me.

230

WHEN THE BATTLE'S OVER

by Harriette Waters, A. E. Lind

And when the battle's over, we shall wear a
  crown!
Yes, we shall wear a crown! Yes, we shall wear
  a crown!
And when the battle's over, we shall wear a
  crown
In the new Jerusalem.
Wear a crown, wear a crown,
Wear a bright and shining crown.
And when the battle's over, we shall wear a
  crown
In the new Jerusalem.

231

**LET GO AND LET GOD
HAVE HIS WAY**

by Harry D. Clarke

Let go and let God have His wonderful way;
Let go and let God have His way.
Your burdens will vanish, your night turn to
  day;
Let go and let God have His way.

232

WHAT A DAY THAT WILL BE

by Jim Hill

What a day that will be
When my Jesus I shall see;
And I look upon His face,
The One who saved me by His grace!

When He takes me by the hand,
And leads me through the promised land;
What a day, glorious day that will be.

233

I HAVE CHRIST IN MY HEART

Not printed due to licensing restrictions.

234

GIVE THEM ALL TO JESUS

by Bob Benson, Sr., Phil Johnson

Give them all, give them all,
Give them all to Jesus:
Shattered dreams, wounded hearts, and
  broken toys.
Give them all, give them all,
Give them all to Jesus;
And He will turn your sorrow into joy!

235

**ONE OF YOUR CHILDREN
NEEDS YOU, LORD**

by Mosie Lister

One of Your children needs You, Lord.
One of Your children needs You, Lord.
One of Your children needs You, Lord.
Jesus, Jesus, be near.

One of Your children is crying, Lord . . .

One of Your children loves You, Lord . . .

236

RIGHT NOW

by Otis Skillings

Right now, right now,
Commit your life right now.
Decide to live your life for Him
Right now, right now.

237

WHERE THE SPIRIT OF THE LORD IS
by Stephen R. Adams

Where the Spirit of the Lord is, there is peace.
Where the Spirit of the Lord is, there is love.
There is comfort in life's darkest hour,
There is light and life;
There is help and power in the Spirit,
In the Spirit of the Lord.

238

NOTHING IS IMPOSSIBLE
by Eugene L. Clark

Nothing is impossible when you put your trust in God;
Nothing is impossible when you're trusting in His Word.
Hearken to the voice of God to thee:
"Is there anything too hard for Me?"
Then put your trust in God alone and rest upon His Word;
For everything, O everything,
Yes, everything is possible with God!

239

MY FAITH STILL HOLDS
by William J. and Gloria Gaither

My faith still holds on to the Christ of Calvary;
Oh, blessed Rock of Ages, cleft for me.
I gladly place my trust in things I cannot see;
My faith still holds on to the Christ of Calvary!

240

GENTLE SHEPHERD
by William J. and Gloria Gaither

Gentle Shepherd, come and lead us,
For we need You to help us find our way.
Gentle Shepherd, come and feed us,
For we need Your strength from day to day.
There's no other we can turn to
Who can help us face another day.
Gentle Shepherd, come and lead us,
For we need You to help us find our way.

241

GREATER IS HE THAT IS IN ME
by Lanny Wolfe

Greater is He that is in me,
Greater is He that is in me,
Greater is He that is in me,
Than he that is in the world!

242

FAITH IN GOD CAN MOVE A MOUNTAIN
by John W. Peterson, Alfred E. Smith

Faith in God can move a mighty mountain,
Faith can calm the troubled sea,
Faith can make the desert like a fountain,
Faith can bring the victory.

243

WE'VE COME THIS FAR BY FAITH
by Albert Goodson

We've come this far by faith,
Leaning on the Lord,
Trusting in His holy Word;
He's never failed us yet.
Oh, we can't turn back;
We've come this far by faith!

244

I BELIEVE THE ANSWER'S ON THE WAY

by Merrill Dunlop

I believe the answer's on the way;
I believe the Lord has heard me pray;
"Cast not away your confidence,"
Saith the Lord our God.
Now by faith in Him alone I stand,
Firmly held by His almighty hand;
Fully trusting in His promise,
Praise the Lord!

245

CARES CHORUS

by Kelly Willard

I cast all my cares upon You.
I lay all of my burdens down at Your feet.
And any time that I don't know what to do,
I will cast all my cares upon You.

246

HE WILL CARRY YOU

by Scott Wesley Brown

There is no problem too big God cannot
solve it.
There is no mountain too tall He cannot
move it.
There is no storm too dark God cannot calm
it.
There is no sorrow too deep He cannot
soothe it.

Refrain:
If He carried the weight of the world upon
His shoulder,
I know, my brother, that He will carry you.
If He carried the weight of the world upon
His shoulder,
I know, my sister, that He will carry you.

He said, "Come unto Me all who are weary
And I will give you rest."
(Repeat 1st 4 lines and refrain)

247

THERE IS A RIVER

by David and Max Sapp

There is a river that flows from deep within;
There is a fountain that frees the soul from
sin.
Come to the water; there is a vast supply.
There is a river that never shall run dry.

248

GOT ANY RIVERS?

by Oscar Eliason

Got any rivers you think are uncrossable?
Got any mountains you can't tunnel through?
God specializes in things thought
impossible—
He does the things others cannot do.

249

IN THE NAME OF THE LORD

by Phil McHugh, Gloria Gaither,
Sandi Patti Helvering

There is strength in the name of the Lord;
There is pow'r in the name of the Lord;
There is hope in the name of the Lord;
Blessed is He who comes in the name of the
Lord.

250

HE IS OUR PEACE

by Kandela Groves

He is our peace, who has broken down every
wall.
He is our peace, He is our peace.
(Repeat)
Cast all your cares on Him, for He cares for
you.
He is our peace, He is our peace.
Cast all your cares on Him, for He cares for
you.
He is our peace, He is our peace.

ALPHABETICAL INDEX

*Indicates titles recorded on the companion split-channel cassette (TA-9102C) and compact disc (DC-9102).